ANIMAL OPPOSITES
HOT AND COLD

by Cecilia Minden

Cherry Lake Publishing • Ann Arbor, Michigan

CHERRY LAKE
Publishing

Published in the United States of America
by Cherry Lake Publishing
Ann Arbor, Michigan
www.cherrylakepublishing.com

Reading Adviser: Marla Conn, ReadAbility, Inc.

Photo Credits: © Anton_Ivanov/Shutterstock Images, cover, 20;
© kminstock/Shuttestock Images, 4; © AnetaPics/Shutterstock Images, 6;
© Darryl Brooks/Shutterstock Images, 8; © Irina Burakova/Shutterstock
Images, 10; © Tungphoto/Shutterstock Images, 12; © AndreAnita/
Shutterstock Images, 14; © Dennis W. Donohue/Shutterstock Images, 16;
© Stephen Lew/Shutterstock Images, 18; © Tati Nova photo Mexico/
Shutterstock Images, 20; © Dan Back Kristensen/Shutterstock Images, 20;
©megastocker/Shutterstock Images, 20

Library of Congress Cataloging-in-Publication Data
Hot and cold / by Cecilia Minden.
    pages cm.—(Animal opposites)
  Audience: K to grade 3.
   ISBN 978-1-63470-473-1 (hardcover)—ISBN 978-1-63470-593-6 (pbk.)—
ISBN 978-1-63470-533-2 (pdf)—ISBN 978-1-63470-653-7 (ebook)
  1. Animals—Juvenile literature. 2. Temperature—Juvenile literature.
3. Concepts—Juvenile literature. 4. Vocabulary. I. Title.
 QL49.M6737 2016
 590—dc23
                                                2015026048

Cherry Lake Publishing would like to acknowledge
the work of the Partnership for 21st Century Skills.
Please visit www.p21.org for more information.

Printed in the United States of America
Corporate Graphics

TABLE OF CONTENTS

Prince of B

Pets

A cat gets tired after playing. It likes to nap in the hot sun.

The dog likes to play in the cold snow.

Farm Animals

This **donkey** lives where it is hot. It eats dry grass.

A **reindeer** lives where it is cold. Its fur protects it from the wind and snow.

What Do You See?

What color is the lizard?

Zoo Animals

The lizard is on the hot rock.
It sits in the sun.

A **polar bear** likes to roll in the snow. It likes the cold.

Water Animals

Alligators live in swamps. The weather is hot there.

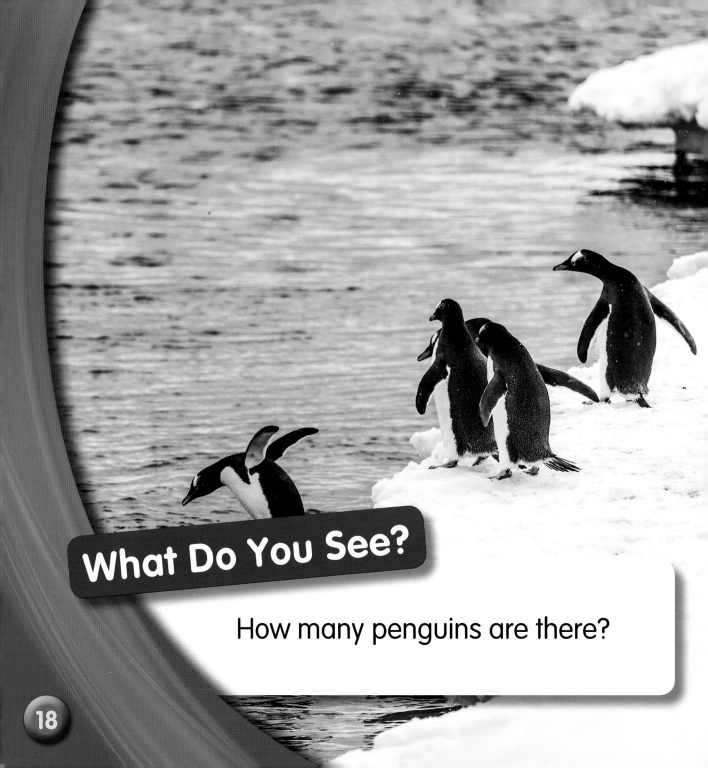

What Do You See?

How many penguins are there?

Penguins like to splash in the cold water. They walk on the cold ice.

Which animals like to be cold?

Which animals like to be hot?

Find Out More

BOOK

Horáček, Petr. *Animal Opposites*. Somerville, MA: Candlewick Press, 2013.

WEB SITE

The Activity Idea Place—Opposites
www.123child.com/lessonplans/other/opposites.php
Play some games to learn even more opposites.

Glossary

donkey (DAHNG-kee) a mammal with long ears that is sometimes used as a work animal

polar bear (POH-lur BAIR) a large bear with thick, white fur that lives in Arctic regions

reindeer (RAYN-deer) a deer with large antlers that lives where it is cold

Home and School Connection

Use this list of words from the book to help your child become a better reader. Word games and writing activities can help beginning readers reinforce literacy skills.

after	hot	sits
alligators	ice	snow
animals	live	splash
are	lizard	sun
cat	many	swamps
cold	nap	the
color	penguins	there
dog	pets	tired
donkey	play	walk
dry	playing	water
eats	polar bear	weather
farm	protects	where
from	reindeer	which
fur	rock	wind
grass	roll	zoo

Index

About the Author

Cecilia Minden, PhD, is a former classroom teacher and university professor. She now enjoys working as an educational consultant and writer for school and library publications. She has written more than 150 books for children. Cecilia lives in and out, up and down, and fast and slow in McKinney, Texas.